THE WARRIOR

ALSO BY FRANCES RICHEY

The Burning Point

THE WARRIOR

Frances Richey

VIKING

VIKING

Published by the Penguin Group

Penguin Group (USA) Inc., 375 Hudson Street,

New York, New York 10014, U.S.A.

Penguin Group (Canada), 90 Eglinton Avenue East, Suite 700,

Toronto, Ontario, Canada M4P 2Y3 (a division of Pearson Penguin Canada Inc.)

Penguin Books Ltd, 80 Strand, London WC2R 0RL, England

Penguin Ireland, 25 St. Stephen's Green, Dublin 2, Ireland (a division of Penguin Books Ltd)

Penguin Books Australia Ltd, 250 Camberwell Road, Camberwell,

Victoria 3124, Australia (a division of Pearson Australia Group Pty Ltd)

Penguin Books India Pvt Ltd, 11 Community Centre,

Panchsheel Park, New Delhi–110 017, India

Penguin Group (NZ), 67 Apollo Drive, Rosedale, North Shore 0632,

New Zealand (a division of Pearson New Zealand Ltd)

Penguin Books (South Africa) (Pty) Ltd, 24 Sturdee Avenue,

Rosebank, Johannesburg 2196, South Africa

Penguin Books Ltd, Registered Offices: 80 Strand, London WC2R 0RL, England

First published in 2008 by Viking Penguin, a member of Penguin Group (USA) Inc.

1 3 5 7 9 10 8 6 4 2

Copyright © Frances Richey, 2008

All rights reserved

Page 83 constitutes an extension of this copyright page.

LIBRARY OF CONGRESS CATALOGING IN PUBLICATION DATA

Richey, Frances.

The warrior / Frances Richey.

p. cm.

ISBN 978-0-670-01961-8

I. Title.

PS3618.I346W37 2008

811'.6—dc22   2007042774

Printed in the United States of America

Set in Dante

Designed by Francesca Belanger

For Ben

CONTENTS

III

IV

I

THE AZTEC EMPIRE

The Guggenheim, 2004

Listen, dearie, there is no world without war.
An unfamiliar voice in my head—
$\qquad\qquad\qquad\qquad$ I stand at the beginning
before stone
plumed serpent, Quetzalcoatl,
celestial being of the dawning east;
wind and breath—beautiful,
if beauty can live where young men die
for kings.
$\qquad\quad$ Does the voice mean
there can only be a world
if there is killing?

My son is in Iraq.
$\qquad\qquad$ I see him
in the faces of soldiers on the news,
in the *Times*—
$\qquad\qquad$ The voice
in my mind, like the tune of a song
I hate but can't forget,
doesn't care about the dark
circles around their eyes
$\qquad\qquad\qquad\qquad$ or about the black alcove;
a stone altar shaped like a bridge,
a slave bent backwards
so the priest could slide a flint knife
into his ribs, extract his beating heart,
a sacrifice
for an Aztec god,
$\qquad\qquad\quad$ the blood caught
in this exquisite bowl behind glass—

red, white, black—glyphs of gold,
the eye of night—
                    The warriors drank from it too,
for land, for women . . .
They used blood the way we use money,
to keep their world going.

Across the spiraled ramp,
an Eagle Warrior:
                    a man's face shadowed
inside a beaked helmet. Slightly bent
at the waist, he could be bowing,
                              if not for the meanness
of his costume: talons
jut from his knees; the stucco edges
of ceremonial feathers spike
at his shoulders—

Before he was a warrior, he was a boy;
before he drank blood, he drank milk. . . .

So what? says the voice. *We're all going to die.*
Who are we to judge?
But I am dizzy, I reply.
Something knocked loose
inside my inner ear,
or perhaps it was the dark body
of the snake.
                    I walked its coil
to the cross of its destroyer.
I had to place my back against a wall
to keep from falling.

THE BARN SWALLOWS

My son is always leaving.
Sometimes he looks back
and waves good-bye. Sometimes
he just disappears.
Where is he now? In the air,
returning from Poland?
On the ground, training at Fort Bragg?
The day he graduated from West Point,
the sun was so bright I couldn't see
the secretary of defense, a dark speck
under the white awning
on a makeshift stage, saying something
about the world, about danger,
a different kind of war.
No one else seemed to notice
the barn swallows swoop in
like a swarm of enormous black butterflies,
their throats bloodied,
marring the brilliance of the sky.
They arrived out of nowhere,
the way my son was suddenly a man.
As each new lieutenant shook
the secretary's hand, the swallows dipped
and keened over the field, the barracks,
those gray castles of learning,
the dead generals bronzed on pedestals.
What had drawn them to this moment,
the red sash and the saber?
What had drawn my son to this life?
Where had it come from,
his certainty of purpose?

When I was my son's age, I had no faith.
Now I believe in the prescience of wings,
each bird, its presentation of colors,
bearing the messages we pray will never come.
Looking down through borrowed binoculars
into the perfect rows,
I searched for his face.

THE MOVERS

Ben said to me once,
You'd better think of something. He meant
he might not always be here.
We stood in his garage and waited for the movers
who had carried all my household goods from storage
in the Bronx to his new house
in Colorado Springs. Soon
we'd watch the chair I rocked him in,
packing paper and tape
hung from it in shreds,
being lifted from the truck
and slowly lowered to the ground. That moment
in the air, it looked like a ghost,
or an old woman's hair,
a small wind blowing through it.

His head was freshly shaved.
A blue square bandage
on his shoulder covered
the small pox shot they all get
before they ship out to Iraq. In days
he'd be cargo on some army plane,
and I'd be in New York City listening
to his message on my machine.
I save all his messages.

Just moved in, he was
still unpacking as he packed
for battle. From his driveway,
rooftops, the Rockies:
solid, immovable, blue,

then slate; they changed
with every subtle shift of light.
A thousand feet into the earth
beneath them, concrete corridors
of NORAD, undetectable
receptors perpetually scanning
air and space, missing nothing—
frosted folds of stone
and snow, peaceful,
as if they drew strength
from staying in one place.

I turned to his yard,
the grass, tentative,
sprouting out of what was once a desert,
made new by banisters and porches,
the faint sound of wind chimes.
He said, *You'd better think of something.*
I said, *I'm trying to think of something,*
though I knew I'd found my work.
I was doing it right there in front of him,
memorizing stubbles of grass
gone dark in twilight,
the green hose coiled on a hook,
his face softening
as the movers pulled a freight
of lifetimes to the curb.

We were turning
into mirrors of ourselves
we didn't know yet,

my son preparing for war,
as I braced myself for months,
years of waiting; and the movers
opening the doors of that truck, their silence
almost reverent. Through the shadows
they filled the yard with boxes:
the dishrags, the iron pots,
a crystal pitcher Hazel gave me
for no reason, the clay sculpture
of a woman grinding corn.

His new life, my old one
intersecting around the steps,
two thousand miles away from
that apartment on Franklin Turnpike
where we moved
the year I lost the house.

He'd cleared a space in his basement
for love letters, stashed in a pillowcase,
from the boy I should have married,
diaries I should have burned.
Books and books and books
scattered in the dusk.

He offered the men water. He stood beside me.
He put the rocker in his den.

LETTERS

1

Before he left for combat,
he took care of everything:
someone to plow the driveway,
cut the grass.
And the letter he wrote me,
just in case, sealed,
somewhere, in a drawer;
can't be opened,
must be opened
if he doesn't return.
I feel for my keys,
hear his voice:
Less is better. Late
for work, still,
I linger
at the window of the Century
Florist, a bowl of peonies,
my face among the tulips.

2

Last Mother's Day, when
he was incommunicado,
nothing came.
Three days later, a message
in my box; a package,
the mail room closed.
I went out into the lobby,
banged my fist against
the desk. When they
gave it to me, I clutched it
to my chest, sobbing
like an animal.
I spoke to no one,
did not apologize.
I didn't care about the gift.
It was the note I wanted,
the salt from his hand,
the words.

THE BOOK OF SECRETS

In his *Secret Book* in second grade, my son wrote:
I hope my mom will get mearyd agen
and I can have a brother or sister. His teacher answered:

I'll hope for you too.
He didn't know she'd give the book to me.
And he was too young to be told

about the child I didn't carry,
there just long enough
to crave cottage cheese and butter.

I was single, in business, a stack
of books beside my bed:
Things Your Mother Never Taught You,

How to Dress for Success. Mornings,
when I left him with the sitter,
I had to close my heart,

or else obsess he was crossing
Oak alone. And I was
pushing it, to show up at his ball games

straight from work, dressed to the teeth,
while the other mothers whispered
in their coveys. The briefcase,

the heels. I was a boss,
and I was bossed,
while they baked pies and waited.

Dusk brought home their men
from the same conference rooms
I lived in sun to sun, numbers

beamed up on a screen so bright
it hypnotized. How could I
give him a brother

or a sister? I was stuck
on the Tappan Zee at rush hour,
watching clouds

foment a woman. From
the waist down, paralyzed, she
slowly dragged herself across the sky.

THE WARRIOR

My students disappear
through glass doors
into their lives.
I stand where I stood
when they were here;
trees, eagles, dancers.
I've turned up the lights,
rolled my mat, gathered
the roster, tissues . . . Someone
forgot a sock. Alone
in the center of the room,
do I have the will
to make a spear of my arms,
expose my heart?

　　　◆ ◆ ◆

It was easy to think of warrior
as a yoga posture, until my son
became a Green Beret. Green:
color of the fourth chakra,
Anahata; it means unstruck—
the heart center—
the color of his fatigues.

When Arjuna rode into battle,
the disguised Krishna by his side,
he looked out from his chariot
over the field of familiar faces,
cried out, *I cannot do this!*
Krishna said, *You must fight!*

Where is the solace in my warrior
if my son is lost?
If he returns another man?

♦ ♦ ♦

1968. Pictures from
My Lai were in the news.
I was too young
to understand what would happen
to the boys I knew
in high school who played
baseball, raised their hands
in Dr. Vahlcamp's lit class;
who met us at the door
with corsages. Boys
in men's bodies, they sat
around a campfire, toasted
marshmallows, drank.
Their gold faces changed
shape in the shimmer
from the flames.

♦ ♦ ♦

Good-bye
to the glistening sand,
waters
that held a thousand doors,
a connection
to life,
warmth, food.

There was a flutter
of lashes, a cradle.
The soft cheek
touching the soft cheek.
Good-bye mother,
father, milk, bread,
petals floating
on the water;
daybreak, nightfall, hawk—
the limp body
of a snake dangling
from its beak. Good-bye
to deciding, arguing, giving up—
hands, feet, all the digits,
pictures, glitter, floorboards,
hair, tears . . .

    ◆ ◆ ◆

My son has brothers now,
the family he wanted. They
share the grueling measure
of his days, this desert war:

twelve around the table,
twelve to make the meal,
twelve to face the danger—
Hung from hooks around
the "ready room," their gear.

    ◆ ◆ ◆

I tell my students, Stand
in your strength

from a place of openness . . .
but none of us has fallen
from the sky, or borne
the cheetah marks of
urban warfare training,
or stanched a wound
while bullets fly.

♦ ♦ ♦

A knot of broad-
shouldered brothers,
they disperse
in the black water
of night—Form
is helpful when
shadows crowd,
and thoughts fly apart.
Something solid.
Something
that can't be broken—
Is it in you, around
you, above you,
below you?
Can you breathe
it in, can you sleep
through it? Can you
tear it with your teeth?
Can you swallow it?
Is it more than you?
Is it you?

IN A TIME OF WAR

After the Guggenheim, El Greco to Picasso

The flayed head of the lamb,
a tooth hanging over its bottom lip,
faces its own butchered loin,
a drooze of blood in the corner
of the one eye open; blood
of the old life drained,
and the new one hidden
in the dark layers behind
the plain pine tabletop
where the bars of the heart
wait to be used for stew.

◆ ◆ ◆

I am not shocked by
the butchered lamb,
not squeamish, as
I would have been
when I was young,
studying for exams,
writing papers for
Dr. Hazelrigg. I was
homesick and sick
of home, against a war
that wasn't real to me,
even when I saw it
in the eyes of boys
who made it
half alive.

◆ ◆ ◆

I walk the coil of this rotunda,
swirl of balconies. From the ram
to the Passion, the bruising ache
of history. I am drawn to the center,
Solana's *Streetwalkers,* those scars
across the cheek and forehead
of the old one in the back.
Beside her the lush,
jaw slack, rheumy eye,
chin jutting forward
as if she's ready
to curse the broken vessels
in her nose—
her breath, the gravel
in her voice. The next one
mannish, her chest a shelf,
shoulders draped in a drab olive robe
stenciled with faded Chinamen.

I love their *fuck you* nonchalance,
their sorrow,
the way they stand together
in that alley against a wall
under the gloomy windows of their village,
their faces the faces of all
who sold themselves: the addict,
the beaten one, the ones without love—
duchesses and devils,
angels and dwarves, my own face
reflected in the glass.
It's the same, the whore

in the center and the holy woman
tending to Saint Sebastian.
The body, stripped
and wounded, makes us weep
and worship. We elevate their suffering,
and our own,
or how could we go on living?

DREAM OF THE LOST SON

Pink walls,
books,
a maple desk.
My girlhood
room, only
I'm middle-aged,
half dressed
in a sweater and slip,
the door closed
while a young man pushes
from the other side.
In his twenties,
light hair,
clean white shirt
and jeans.
He could break
in if he wanted.
He's that other child,
the one I didn't have—
Summer
beside a wagon wheel
abandoned in a field.
A girl, I imagined,
as I signed the papers
at that clinic
in Bridgeport. He asks
for nothing.

II

KILL SCHOOL

That was the summer he rappelled
down mountains on rope

that from a distance looked thin
as the dragline of a spider,

barely visible, the tension
he descended

into the made-up
state of Pineland

with soldiers from his class.
They started with a rabbit,

and since my son was the only one
who'd never hunted,

he went first. He described it:
moonlight, the softness

of fur, another pulse
against his chest.

The trainer showed him
how to rock the rabbit

like a baby in his arms,
faster and faster,

until every sinew surrendered
and he smashed its head into a tree.

They make a little squeaking sound,
he said. *They cry.*

He drove as he told me:
You said you wanted to know.

I didn't ask how he felt.
Maybe I should have,

but I was biting
off the skin from my lips,

looking out
beyond the glittering line

of traffic flying
past us in the dark.

WAITING

In my dream a girl
floats on a raft.
She bends,
pulls from the river
a small, dark
winged thing,
brings it to me,
a stone, John
(my son's first name,
the one we never use)
chiseled into it.
I'm half awake:
5:15 A.M.; 1:15 P.M. in Iraq

        ♦ ♦ ♦

On the way to the doctor,
I carry the dream in my body
over the snowy walk
past Wollman Rink . . .
8 A.M.; 4 P.M. in Iraq

Ben has asked for warm clothes,
lip balm. I'd forgotten
it could get cold in the desert.

      In the beginning,
all the stories were about
the heat, anguished
faces; that Iraqi man
on his knees, caught
in crossfire, the futile container

his arms were
around his small son.

♦ ♦ ♦

9 A.M.; 5 P.M. *in Iraq*
As the cold dime of
the stethoscope sweeps
my back, I imagine Ben
underground in a
concrete room, maps
spread out on tables,
tacked to walls. He moves
from map to map,
never leaves the room.
This is how I keep him safe.

♦ ♦ ♦

The vertigo started in March
when he told me
he would be deployed.
I sat down on the sidewalk
at the corner of Forty-third
and Broadway, waited
for the spinning to stop.

12 P.M.; 8 P.M. *in Iraq*
The technician gives
me earplugs, presses
the button that slides
my body into the white
tunnel, where harsh

knocks and alarms
hammer out the map
of my brain, hidden
in its burning pigments,
the memory of my son
when he was three, sitting
by a window, waiting for
the rain to stop so
we could walk through
the mud to the lake
where we would place
our hands on stones,
let ladybugs crawl all over them.

          ◆ ◆ ◆

I believed if I was present
for his football games,
he wouldn't get hurt;
that if I made the two-hour drive
from Stamford to Ramsey
in half the time
that day he ran into a tree,
I could keep him
whole in his body.

Midafternoon, September,
after Beast, that first
training plebe year, I fixed
him in my mind,
and he called
later that evening: *Mom,*

were you at West Point today?
And I said no.
                    But I thought
I saw you on the Plain.
I said no, but what time
did you see me?
And he named the moment
I'd prayed for him.

I thought it had something
to do with our
heartbeats, like clocks
placed in the same
room. Once

I believed I could
close my eyes and know,
even when my son was
on the other side of the world,
if he was alive.

ONE WEEK BEFORE DEPLOYMENT

1—Packing

There was something about
the helmet, in a pile
of gear by the fireplace. Once
another soldier's, now my son's,
it called to me the way the dying do
when they can no longer speak;
an irresistible pull, like gravity
or love.
       I wanted to touch it.

   ◆ ◆ ◆

Two pairs of desert camo boots
stood beside the black recliner.
They shouldn't have been
beautiful, shimmering
like suede, lightweight
for easy movement, never worn.
A man can't wear another man's boots.
They mold to his feet,
carry his scent, his sweat
absorbed in the hide.
They take on the shape
of his bunions, his burdens,
the soles worn down
with his rhythms,
his weight when he walks.

   ◆ ◆ ◆

I've seen pictures of those
makeshift totems in the desert.

They call the name out three times;
three times, the silence,
a pair of boots
beside a rifle, its nose in the sand,
the barrel standing
for the soft ribs of a body.

2—To the Helmet

                        Ghost
of a moon half draped
in the folds of his rain poncho,
how many have died
because you weren't enough?
Because you couldn't be everywhere?
I wanted to put you on,
but you weren't mine, your only
country that remnant
of the fontanel I felt once
while he slept
before the bones closed over it.

3—His Gun

I looked for it
the way I looked
for that rattler
in the field
when I was
small. Dark
diamonds,
beautiful,
shed skin
a shadow
in the basket
among sheets
and clothespins.

      ◆ ◆ ◆

He left it out
of sight, as if recalling
my refusal,
when he was a boy,
to buy him one.
The only evidence
it existed, a small
brown square of paper,
slightly buckled,
three holes shot
through at the heart,
lying on the table
by his will.

◆ ◆ ◆

I must have seemed
a hypocrite that winter
I visited him
in Bamburg, his first
command, and asked
to watch him practice
on the range. He said
he'd rather not,
and when I pressed—
It's not my gun—
meaning, I suppose,
he didn't choose it,
didn't love it, one
more possession,
government issue,
passed from
hand to hand.

◆ ◆ ◆

It wasn't about blood
or necessity, it wasn't
about love—or
maybe it was
all of these that drove
my desire to see
how he carried it,
if he cradled it,
how it fit against

his body, to see
the side he hides
from me, the dark
beauty.

4—Sightseeing

Ben and Marsha took me to
the Garden of the Gods.
I picked up small rocks on the path.
The red rubbed off
on my fingers like chalk.
Is that all the gods are made of?

Ben sat under an enormous boulder
supported by one
small fulcrum of stone.
His tiny form under its shade
made a good picture.
No one seemed concerned
the boulder could fall.

♦ ♦ ♦

We drove up Pikes Peak.
Our ears popped.
Ben played the sound track
from *The Passion*. I was afraid
the thin air would take my breath.
When he was small, asthmatic,
we made midnight runs
for Adrenalin.
                    Even then,
he wasn't scared,
                    just a little *uneasy*.
It was so quiet
at the top, I didn't want to leave.

A couple with a new baby got out of a Jeep.
I helped the man pull
his daughter's tiny legs through holes
in the infant knapsack.
Halfway down the mountain, I thought
the baby's lungs
                        might be too fragile
                                        for the altitude,
too late
to go back and warn them.

5—I Had Promised Not to Cry

He had his mission to think about,
his men.
                    I asked him
to go through the blue folder with me,
his vaccinations,
ID cards, Hazardous Duty Orders . . .
I told myself this would bring us closer.
That was a lie.
                    It gave me distance,
like the scientist
who examines every detail
through a lens.

6—Inventory

2 pairs desert camo boots
sleeping bag
salt pack: Nods, ammo, night-vision goggles
wind-stopper gloves

These don't belong to me.

camelback backpack for water
Kevlar helmet
mich helmet
grenade pouches
magazine pouches

I have no place here. This is not my life.

green laser
equipment vest
9-millimeter holster
same old ruck

*He can't bear my worry. Like the rucksack he carries on his back, it
seems to suck the life out of him.*

socks . . . green/black
PTs—shorts, shirts for workout
Spears silk underwear for cold weather
Spears body armor . . . ergonomically correct
barracks bag for laundry

rain poncho and liner
black wool cap

I was always asking if he was warm enough.
Put a sweater on, I'd say. Your jacket . . .

duffel bag
entrenching tool
knee pads
elbow pads
uniforms
Nuclear, Biological, Chemical suit

I can't protect him.

Vaccinations:
anthrax
hepatitis
flu shot
meningitis
tetanus
typhoid
smallpox
TD

No one could explain his nosebleeds. They always seemed to come when I
was packing for business trips: Pittsburgh, Chicago, Detroit . . .

CDs: Springsteen, Sarah McLachlan, U2 . . .
DVDs: *In the Name of the Father, Boondock Saints, Elf . . .*

Marlboros
Chewing tobacco

Tissues fell from him like crumpled doves.

Pin light
Case for Christ
Onward Muslim Soldier
Salem's Lot
Catcher in the Rye
Laminated four-leaf clover

*He tilted his head back, pinched his nose between thumb and index
finger: "Don't worry, I know what to do."*

Officer Record Brief
Hazardous Duty Orders
Zero Your Weapon

He's given me his dog-eared copy of Komunyakaa's
Neon Vernacular, *underlined:*
"We can transplant broken hearts/
but can we put goodness back into them?"

Life Insurance: To be split between Mom and Dad
Emergency Records . . . Who gets called
Battalion wants to know what to read
at your funeral, what songs to play . . .

He looks up from the paperwork
hard into my eyes:
"You said you wanted to know."

THETIS

Her son was going to do
what he was going to do.
He was headstrong and beautiful

and couldn't imagine
he would ever die. From
where she slept in the depths

of the sea, she heard his cry
and did what sons despise:

she intervened,

commissioned divine armor,
lobbied Zeus. . . .
It's the same

when you see your son fall
in with a bad crowd:
he's thirteen and won't listen,

so you stop by the school
on your way home from work,
tell the principal, and quietly,

he takes an interest in the boy.

Isn't that your job?
To whisper in the ear of
any god who'll listen: *Please,
protect him.*

III

MOURNING IN SADR CITY

After Adilal-Khazali's photograph of five Iraqi women grieving
next to the coffin of a child killed in a string of mortar attacks,
The New York Times, *May 2, 2007*

When I hold the loupe over
their faces, no question which one
is the mother. She lies
on her side in the dirt, shrouded
in the dark robe of the poor,
her face almost peaceful
as if she too has died.
The others, weeping, tilt
in her direction— All that black,
like a fury, bleeds
around the lidless box; splintered
slats of wood thrown
together so quickly,
they don't meet at the corners.
Inside, the lost child, wrapped
in white embroidered cloth,
seems to shine
through the threads. The woman
in the foreground holds
an infant the way a bride
would carry her bouquet,
a measured distance from her waist
as if this beauty too
will perish.
           Ink from their robes
rubs off on my hands.

with so little time, he paces
outside the planetarium
while I rest on a slate bench.
It has rained all morning, cutting
the brutal heat.
          His face
is still beautiful, more serious;
his shoulders built up. He shakes
his head and says
I use the word "brutal" too easily.

          He has another life
where he stuffs a plug of tobacco
inside his cheek, straps a knife
to his thigh, searches
the homes of strangers, alert
to anything that moves. In that life
he knows the difference between
killing and murder, that even
though the children are frightened,
he must keep his helmet on.

     ◆ ◆ ◆

He buys our tickets
as if I were the child, ushers me
to the second floor, where we disappear
into galaxies, vast
and moving too fast to take notes.
From the moment he arrived,
all he wanted was to enter this sphere
together, to fumble for seats, indistinguishable

from the others in the black bowl of a sky
not yet turned on.

            A voice in the dome
tells us behind each star we can see,
the night hides millions more,
like the words we don't say
behind the ones we use to
get through moments like this when
too much time has passed between us
and every visit could be the last.

        ◆ ◆ ◆

What is a star?
Just another body that will live
and die driven by fire? Who dreamed it
into life before space
gave it a home? Questions
a mother doesn't think to ask
as her small son
                points to its shining.

Above us
hunters and heroes
morph into necklaces strung
from carbon and dust. They spiral
farther and farther away. We can't
touch them. We can't touch
any of them, though the voice says
every atom of oxygen we breathe
was made inside a star.

◆ ◆ ◆

If they're in our blood,
why must they be so distant?
I don't know where he's going
or how far apart we might drift.

        Our seats rumble.
The earth whirls through us.
He will leave again.
Again, I'll be broken, a relic
of that young woman I was when
I stood over his bassinet and
hoped his rash would heal
if I changed to cloth.

HE TELLS EACH STORY

with his hands, all the lines
in his palms deeply creased.
When he makes his right
a gun, it is a gun;
the third and index fingers
fused, extended;
the thumb bent sharp
at the knuckle. Sometimes
his left hand hovers
over his chest,
as if he still wears armor,
as if his heart must be
protected from his touch.

SCHOOL FOR COMMANDOS

He says he's learned to pit a car.
When I ask what he means, he opens up
his laptop, clicks a square. It bursts
into sound: A black car rams
the left rear fender of another
black car, which skids
into a spin: Driving School
for Commandos: a thousand
orange cones he has to weave
at the speed of light. He clicks
the next square, next lesson:
a single careless moment
costs a life—
We watch a cabbie caught
on cab-cam, with only
one hand on the
wheel (the way
he's always driven),
startle awake, his body
yanked from side to side,
his eyes wide.
We watch him die:
propelled up,
then swiftly back and
halfway out the right rear
window. He never
brings his right hand to the wheel.
So many squares Ben takes
into his body. The sky
is gray, the ground is gray,
the hand and arm rotting

in the road, gray. I pass
on the others waiting to be opened
like dreams the dreamer doesn't know
he's dreaming. And though I grab
his shoulders with both hands
when we say good-bye
at the airport in Chicago, already
he's giving up everything
to the next moment.
Last night I dreamed I wrapped
my right leg around the back
of my head and
told my horrified lunch date:
You just have to round your spine
a little and bend your knee, then went on
with my story.

A WALK THROUGH
THE SEVENTH REGIMENT ARMORY

A dim glow burns
in the northern corridor: forty-eight stars,
the first stripe ripped;
a jagged wound lets
in what light there is . . . and another
in the next stripe,
and another like a hand
reaching into the blue; a window
of absence in the seventh
and eighth, the torn piece
hangs like a tent flap. . . .
You can see the places
where it was patched,
so much at stake
for the men who carried it
in all its ruin.
              Soldiers
on the walls in their dark
oils stare through the lace
of a Union flag, black
as a widow's bonnet,
held together with blood
and dust, its tassels haunting
as Ben's words
this last time he returned
from the field:
              It wouldn't matter
if an enemy burned the flag in front of me,
it is seared into my heart.
              I bow
to the staff of a regiment flag,

a ripple of smoke, the singed braid—
Whatever is left,
they bring it back, hang it
in a hall like this,
above the fading
medals of honor, accordion gates
to keep us out.
I feel sick to my stomach,
face-to-face with the gallantry
of men young
as my son when they served,
their ribbons bequeathed to these airless
walls where they rest unseen.

CAB RIDE TO CHELSEA

Moaze—that's his name.
Moaze Abbas. *Abbas is like Smith,*
he says. *But Moaze is the name of*
a great teacher who accompanied
Mohammed. Who is this soft-
spoken boy winding his way through
the crooked streets of the Village?
This man. Where is his mother?
She's still there. . . .
But I've been able to bring over a brother.

THE WORST THING

. . . too many windows and doors.
You have to check each one: look through it,
around it, beyond it . . .

♦ ♦ ♦

You have to use the light
on your gun. That shadow
in the corner, a bad guy
can move around inside it.

♦ ♦ ♦

When you're attacked,
you've got three to five seconds
to make the right move.
Guys get killed in the open,
when they should jump
behind a wheel well.
That's why they shoot us
again and again
with plastic bullets for mistakes
the body makes, until it learns
to override the monkey—
adrenaline. When it's pumped,
you'll do things you'd never do at home.

♦ ♦ ♦

360-degree security. Crucial.
If you're not sure, you have to call out
to the rear: "Are you there?"
The whole James Bond thing looks glamorous
in film, but let me tell you, the worst thing,
the worst, is to be out there alone.

CHRISTMAS DINNER WITH MY SON
IN ARLINGTON HEIGHTS

1

Drunk, he makes a book of his hands,
brings his palms together, opens them
to turn each page. *Here,* he says,
have a good look at all our secrets.

He's wearing that blue satin Santa hat
with the New York Giants logo, a fake
fur trim around his flushed face:
Affirmative Action's had its day . . .
I say I needed it to support us. It hurts

to be mad at him. He's due to redeploy.
Thirty years ago, for one terrifying moment,
he was tugged back
by the tangled cord. And how he did it,
I don't know, he fought his way
through the barrier between that life and this . . .

Do you know why I became a Green Beret?
Because I wanted to punish those guys
who beat you down at work
and when you tried to buy a car . . .

2

Trudy worries about Muffy.
She's afraid Muff is going to be eaten
by coyotes. She says a neighbor dog
was eaten by a pack, or maybe only one.

She's not sure.
I say: This is Arlington Heights.
Where do they live?
On the golf course.
Where did they come from?
They've always been here.

3

Buzz is passed out on the couch
in the Christmas room,
his arms across his chest.
Scott skulks around.
Hung on the pale
green wall behind my son,
a department store copy
of Wyeth's golden, Nell,
her luminous head heavy
against a feed sack,
on her face a look so strange
Wyeth wondered if it was her.

4

The moment he was born, I saw
my body open, his dark crown wet
as feathers, the globes of his shoulders . . .
And what had been a private dream
inside me, trembled

from a stranger's hand, suddenly
and utterly alive.

He lists in his chair,
rests his left ear on his shoulder, squints
as if straining to hear some distant chord:

There are things I will never be able to tell you.

5

*I will crush you
and everyone like you!*

Everywhere he goes, he's in the field.

If I could take that hat off his head,
he wouldn't say those things.

IV

E-MAIL FROM A SECRET LOCATION IN IRAQ:
RE: THE PUPPIES

Here are some pictures of the girls. They're a little dirty
from chasing cows away from the trash pile.

I click on the puppies,
their noses smudged with dirt.
They play-fight;
take each other's legs
and tails into their mouths.
They don't bear down.
They have no sense of lastness.
Work will come later: Farm dogs?
Guard dogs?
Trained to sniff out mines?

Beyond the frame, there are cows,
which suggests a pasture,
chickens maybe, eggs.
There could be a garden,
vegetables, staked vines.
And a house with room enough
for ten or twelve men
who call it "home," sleep,
cook, play cards.
On missions, they're "away,"
whatever it is they do,
a mystery
that must remain a mystery.

        ◆ ◆ ◆

When my son was small,
I set boundaries: first the yard,
then our street, our block.

Later, lost
on a back road in Virginia,
I let him take the wheel, dark
but for the car's high beams,
a few stars. He told me:
I want to be a soldier.
I thought he'd change
his mind, just fifteen,
his future as invisible
as the fields we passed.
I was happy for the sound
our words made on the air.

Will he come back?

    ◆ ◆ ◆

I print the puppies out, fold them
into my days, motherless,
nameless—
Call them joy's wild sisters.
Call them glory.
Call them love's hidden window
in a burning world.

He's shot each picture from above,
betrayed nothing
of the place. One pup
rests her chin on his knee,
her ears laid back
and down against her head,
her mouth slightly open, whiskers

so still they tremble,
the way the lashes of the dead
seem to move. I am struck
by the decency of sunlight, his hand
on her head, light passing
through that touch,
the gold hairs on his arm,
her gold fur . . . I look
and look as if by looking
I can keep them in the world.

TIME OUT

I don't remember what he'd done.
He was two. He'd done something,
and I'd read that instead of spanking,
you could put your child in a chair
and tell him to sit there and think
about what he'd done. A mother
mothered by a woman who could not
control her rages, I was determined
not to hit him. Sit here, I said, and
put him in the little wooden chair
in the corner of his room beside the
window. Maybe he was three. All
arms and legs, he fought me. Think,
I said, as I ran for the door, closed it,
and held it closed, while he pulled
with all his strength on the other side,
Think about what you've done.

THE POWERLIFTER

Arvin Gym, West Point, 1998

The doors swung open on the smell of baby
powder, sweat and chalk—
Disks of steel crashed
to the court, their thunder echoing
from the high beams down
through the bleachers where
the fathers receded
on the sidelines, and the mothers,
like nervous schoolgirls, laughed,
gossiped, while they waited for their sons
to take the floor.

Jean Good, whose shoulders I rubbed that night,
is dead. She wore a wig, her hair
just growing back from chemo.
She wanted to live
through Ring Weekend,
her son's graduation.

Most of them too small
to be football players for Army—
they were the powerlifters,
full of combustion, desire
to show someone:
a father? a mother? they could
carry the whole goddamn family
on their backs.

One kid's pec split open on a lift.
Another broke his wrist. I watched
my son deadlift

five hundred pounds, drag the bar
up his powdered legs,
right palm up—left palm down,
the lock,
his face red and twisted

as it was the night his father left:
he pulled himself up,
gripped the bars of his crib,
refused to be held.

He'd asked us both to be there:
his father smoked at the gym door;
I held hands with Jean
and screamed his name.

He got a rush from it,
but his eyes bled,
and he wouldn't stop,
his body his to sacrifice.

I didn't look away.
It would have been betrayal—
The hours he'd spent building
his tolerance for pain—
He was prepared, right there,
in the middle of the gym,
to crush his heart.

THOR

1

Wild dogs, he said. I got caught up
with some wild dogs.
They were out hunting . . .
He sits beside me in the garden
behind his building,
                              so young
to know what he knows.
I walked up a dirt mound,
                    on the other side,
a wild dog
staring me in the face,
                    oil burning,
this big tanker going up in the air . . .
                              A horse
lying in a ditch,
its backside eaten . . .

                    I keep looking
at that tattoo inside his right forearm,
a whacked-out doll: one eye x'd out,
the other, a crazy wheel of rays.
                              He was drunk—
a hatpin through its heart,
                              that doll,
the only one he wanted.

                    Yes.
but what about the dog?
What happened to the dog?

                    Wild dogs,
he said. That was it, what stuck
in his head;
                    and the dead bodies,
the burnt flesh . . .
a rotten, rubbery,
                    carcassy smell . . .

Still that smell is in me.

2

I wonder if it did
affect me a little.
                    When I watch movies
like Black Hawk Down
and they play that music, my heart
starts pumping . . .
                    He makes the sound
of the singing, a high-pitched
            AAAhaaahAAAhaaahAAA . . .

Shrapnel in it,
                    torches,
the last whispered wishes
of the dead.

            I saw a woman in Old Navy.
She was dressed up like they were,
all black, and the gloves . . .

She was young.
She must have lost a husband
or done something bad . . . the gloves.

I started sweating . . .
Not that I didn't trust that woman . . .
but I didn't.

INCOMMUNICADO

Love you. That's how she knows
his girlfriend didn't send
the gift for Mother's Day.
If it had said, Lots of love,
or You're the best,
she would have known
it wasn't him. *Love you*
lasered on a plain white card
in the basket of sponges
and candles, bath beads,
teas with names like Zen
and Calm, Tranquillity.
He's incommunicado.
She's been instructed to stop
sending packages
and letters. He's leapt
into the ether, where all things
go that vanish. Nowhere
and everywhere,
a mountain cave, the Tigris
—*Love you*—
on her mind, in her heart,
in the shoulders of the sailor
she follows for a block.
He's incommunicado,
a Greenie floating
over fields and fires
or melted into sand
with other Greenies: wrapped
in scarves, or bald,
or with a beard—like Krishna,

hidden under robes —
He could be anywhere,
anyone—
that's what happens
when you vanish,
you become ubiquitous:
a ghost—a god.

COLLISIONS

to my son in Iraq

There's a new space show
at the Rose Center.
It's all about collisions,
how one little particle, or
cosmic rock thrown
off course, can make
a moon, or tilt a planet
into life. And though
I felt comforted among
the stars you love,
I'm beginning to accept
we're never safe,
the universe always
in motion, even when
we sleep, particles
making and remaking
our bodies, the world
between us a fire
that burns away
the planks of the heart.
I don't know how
they calibrated those
holographic comets and
asteroids with the
thunder of impact,
each explosion just
bearable. I tensed up
anyway, as I do
when cars and trucks
blow up on the news.
I almost closed my eyes,

but I could feel you
in the empty seat
beside me, shake
your head and say,
You're too timid,
the way you did when
you were twelve
and I was afraid to open
the door I'd forgotten
to lock. You
went in ahead of me.

FOUR FRAGMENTS FROM
THE HALL OF THE MADONNAS

The Metropolitan Museum of Art

It's overwhelming, all the little mothers
lined up on the walls: red and black
and gold and gold and gold!
Each with her boy,
her damaged frame
burnt by the worshipper's
candles, their careless longing.

    ◆ ◆ ◆

Nights I hurried down
the hallway to his room,
stood still in the dark
by his crib,
listening.

    ◆ ◆ ◆

Suffering done right is quiet:
a crack in the marble,
the crumbling throne. That fly
on the low stone ledge separates
the nursing mother
from the prophet, who waits
in the wilderness, living
off locusts and wild honey.

    ◆ ◆ ◆

Little swarm of angels,
from the manger to the cross,
like hummingbirds, catch,

in small gold cups,
every drop of his blood.
It is, I suppose, a glorious story,
as long as it's *her* son.

THE CANAL

Home to carp, fallen leaves,
their crisp veins melted
                into the murky mirror.
        One of the lake's long fingers
licking back
                below an underpass into our midst.
        Catcher of seeds and insects,
feathers and clouds, the face of my boy,

        barely three, belly down
on the worn planks of the dock,
                swirling a stick—
        stirring up something—
Then, the water opening,
                taking him,
        closing over his head
as if nothing had happened.

        I looked up from my book
into his absence—
        What is it called
        when the body takes over,
pumps the legs
                to the right spot,
        plunges the arms
down through the surface,

        trusting the hands to haul him up
swaddled in slime,
                still holding his breath—
        all the life he's kept from the water

loosed in one fevered shriek?
        God can be whatever you want,
      a broken mirror
that sees all aspects at once:

    the fearless child,
the mother distracted, the loneliness
        of the water.
    Thank God for the circles, still visible,
the center discernible.
        Thank God
      for good hearing, strong legs.
I carried him shivering

    into the house,
lathered his mottled shoulders
        and belly,
    shampooed the cap
of silt from his hair,
        little body,
      wet in my arms,
twice born.

NOTES

"Letters": I am indebted to Erika Kingetsu, whose gift of an omamori gave this poem its beginning; and to Kenny Jones, security guard, who secured the key.

"The Warrior": I found the phrase "the ready room," in Dana Priest's book *The Mission*. Also, the first five italicized lines of the last stanza in this poem, beginning with "*A knot of broad-shouldered brothers,*" are paraphrased from the same book.

"Inventory": "Zero Your Weapon" means aligning the weapon sights with the point of impact. When a soldier receives a weapon he or she has not fired before, the sights are set for the previous user, or may not be set at all (mechanical zero). Through a series of three-round shot groups, the shooter adjusts the front (elevation) and rear (left/right) sights to put five out of six consecutive rounds inside a four-centimeter circle from a distance of twenty-five meters.

The lines quoted from Yusef Komunyakaa's book *Neon Vernacular* are from the poem "1984," which originally appeared in his collection *I Apologize for the Eyes in My Head*.

"Thetis": In Greek mythology, Thetis is a sea nymph. She is immortal, and one of the fifty Nereids, daughters of "the ancient one of the seas." She is the mother of Achilles by Peleus, king of the Myrmidons of Thessaly.

"Thor": Thor Swetnam was a medic in the first surge to Baghdad in 2003, Third Brigade, Third ID. He treated wounded Iraqi civilians and American soldiers. Though he fought and patrolled in a flak vest that didn't work, he made it home. This poem is dedicated to his mother, Kenetta Swetnam.

During the writing of these poems, I found the following books indispensable for a better understanding of the lives of soldiers in combat:

The Mission: Waging War and Keeping Peace with America's Military, Dana Priest (W. W. Norton & Co., 2003)

The Things They Carried, Tim O'Brien (Houghton Mifflin, 1990)

On Killing: The Psychological Cost of Learning to Kill in War and Society, Lt. Col. Dave Grossman (Back Bay Books / Little, Brown & Co., 1995)

Masters of Chaos, Linda Robinson (PublicAffairs, 2004)

ACKNOWLEDGMENTS

Grateful acknowledgment is made to the editors of the following journals, where some of these poems, sometimes in earlier versions, appeared. *Bellevue Literary Review:* "The Barn Swallows"; *Gulf Coast:* "Kill School," "Waiting," "Home on Leave"; *Heliotrope:* "The Canal"; *River Styx:* "Collisions" appeared as "To My Son in Iraq"; *Upstreet:* "His Gun," "He Tells Each Story," "The Powerlifter"; *Dogwood:* "E-mail from a Secret Location in Iraq: Re: The Puppies"; *The New York Times:* "Letters" (part 2); *Salamander:* "Time Out"; "The Barn Swallows" was reprinted in *The Buffalo News,* Buffalo, New York, November 30, 2004. "Collisions," first published as "To My Son in Iraq," won second place in the *River Styx* International Poetry Contest and was featured online as a selection in *Verse Daily,* January 7, 2007. Part 2 of "Letters" was selected by Nicholas Kristof for publication in his op-ed column "The Poets of War" in *The New York Times,* June 11, 2007. "Waiting" and "Kill School" were reprinted in *O: The Oprah Magazine,* November 2007.

Many people have blessed this book with their love, encouragement, material support, and inspiration. I am deeply grateful to Ben Richey; Trudy Richey; my brilliant agent, Molly Friedrich; the ever thoughtful and resourceful Jacobia Dahm; Paul Cirone; and, at Viking Penguin, Clare Ferraro; my editor, Paul Slovak, whose wisdom and guidance have given me heart; Francesca Belanger; Katherine Griggs; Carolyn Coleburn; Nancy Sheppard; Maggie Payette; Lindsay Prevette; Kate Lloyd; Kelly Blair; Maureen Sugden; Susan Johnson; Andrew Duncan; David Martin; and Courtney Greenwald. I wish to thank Amy Gross, Catherine Kelley, Brooke Glassberg, and the terrific staff at *O: The Oprah*

Magazine; and, at WNET Channel Thirteen, John DeNatale and Bob Morris. My heartfelt thanks also to Alison Jarvis, Michael Fisher, Holly Carter, Thor Swetnam, Gloria Steinem, Melissa Bank, Lisa Wolfe, Stephen Dubner, Shirley Ross, Zoe Sheehan Soldana, Donna Masini, Marie Howe, Leisha Douglas, Jo Brown, Haena Park, June Stein, M. A. Rocks, Sally Bliumis, Nancy Burstein, Marianna Sabater, Violaine Bernbach, Danielle Ofri, Stacy Bodziak, Corie Feiner, and all my friends and colleagues at *Bellevue Literary Review.*

I am forever indebted to two very special women: to Judy Katz for the generous gift of studio space where so many of these poems were written, for her sage counsel and incomparable vision, and for every door and window she has opened to me year after year; and to Rita Gabis, esteemed first reader, friend, and mentor, for her compassion, patience, and superb editorial suggestions.

Finally, special thanks to everyone at Hedgebrook for providing me with a transcendent residency where this book was completed.